LOS CAMPESINOS
FARMWORKERS

MARÍA L. VILLAGÓMEZ VICTORIA

Balboa Press books may be ordered through booksellers or by contacting:

Balboa Press
A Division of Hay House
1663 Liberty Drive
Bloomington, IN 47403
www.balboapress.com
1 (877) 407-4847

ISBN: 978-1-9822-3016-6 (sc)
ISBN: 978-1-9822-3017-3 (e)

Library of Congress Control Number: 2019908296

Print information available on the last page.

Balboa Press rev. date: 07/31/2019

BALBOA.
PRESS
A DIVISION OF HAY HOUSE

Dedicatoria: Este libro se lo dedico a mi mamá y a mis tías. Ellas trabajaron *piscando* fresa en Oxnard, California por muchos años en los años 70s y 80s. Eran unas de las mejores. A veces, *piscaban* más de 110 cajas por día.

Dedication: This book is dedicated to my mother and my aunts. They picked strawberries in Oxnard, California for many years in the 70s and 80s. Also, they were some of the fastest pickers. Sometimes, they would pick more than 110 boxes per day.

Los campesinos son muy trabajadores. A veces, trabajan hasta doce horas por día recogiendo frutas y verduras que nosotros podemos disfrutar en nuestras comidas.

Farmworkers are hardworking people. Sometimes, they work up to twelve hours per day picking fruits and vegetables that we can enjoy in our meals.

Casi siempre, los campesinos trabajan bajo un
sol ardiente. Tiene que cubrirse muy bien del sol
y tomar mucha agua para seguir trabajando.

*Almost always, farmworkers work under a very strong
sun. They must cover up to protect themselves from the
sun and must drink a lot of water to continue working.*

Muchos campesinos van de lugar a lugar siguiendo las cosechas como las fresas, el chile y el algodón en el sur de California, las cerezas y las manzanas en Washington o uva de mesa en el Valle de Napa.

Many farmworkers go from place to place following harvests such as the strawberry, pepper and cotton harvests in southern, California, the cherry and the apple harvests in Washington or the grape harvest in the Napa Valley.

Muchos campesinos tienen que dejar a sus familias en otros lugares para poder trabajar en un lugar distante.

Many farmworkers must leave their families behind in a different location in order to be able to work in a faraway place.

Cuando no existían los teléfonos inteligentes, muchos campesinos les escribían cartas a sus familias para mantenerse en contacto.

Before we had Smart phones, many farmworkers would write letters to their families to stay in contact.

A veces, les llamaban por teléfono. Las familias que no tenían teléfono tenían que usar el teléfono de algún vecino para comunicarse con sus familias.

Sometimes, they would call their families by phone. Families who didn't have a phone would have to borrow their neighbor's phone to communicate with their families.

Muchos campesinos que siguen las cosechas no pueden ver a sus familias con frecuencia, pero sí las extrañan.

Many farmworkers who follow harvests do not get to see their families often, but they do miss them.

Y tú, ¿cuánto tiempo pasas sin ver o hablar con tus papás? ¿Te imaginas si no pudieras verlos todos los días? ¿Cómo te sentirías?

And you, do you get to see or speak to your parents every day? Can you imagine if you couldn't see your parents every day? How would that make you feel?

Los campesinos llegan cansados de trabajar.
Pero de todas maneras juegan con sus
hijos cuando llegan del trabajo.

*Farmworkers are tired when they get home. But
they still wish to play with their kids after work.*

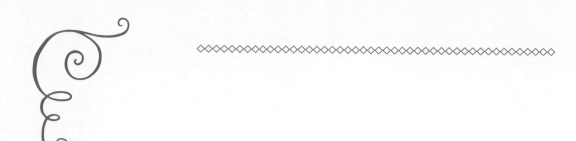

En la vida de los campesinos, muchas veces
los hijos mayores tienen que ayudar a sus
papás en la casa a cuidar a sus hermanos.

*In the lives of farmworkers, many times the oldest child
must help his or her parents take care of his or her siblings.*

¿Conoces a un campesino o a una campesina? Pregúntale de su trabajo. Quizás te sorprenda lo que te cuenten.

Do you know a farmworker? Ask him or her about their work. Their story might surprise you.

Printed in the United States
By Bookmasters